Edward Beckham

A Brief Discovery of Some of the Blasphemous

and seditious principles and practices of the people, called Quakers : taken

out of their most noted and approved authors. Humbly offered to the

consideration of the King, and both houses of Parliament

Edward Beckham

A Brief Discovery of Some of the Blasphemous
*and seditious principles and practices of the people, called Quakers : taken out of
their most noted and approved authors. Humbly offered to the consideration of the
King, and both houses of Parliament*

ISBN/EAN: 9783337410834

Printed in Europe, USA, Canada, Australia, Japan

Cover: Foto ©Lupo / pixelio.de

More available books at **www.hansebooks.com**

A Brief

DISCOVERY

Of SOME of the

Blasphemous and *Seditious*

Principles and Practices

Of the People, Called

QUAKERS:

Taken out of their

Most Noted and Approved Authors.

Humbly Offered to the Consideration of the KING, *and both Houses of* PARLIAMENT.

BY

Edward Beekham D. D. and Rector of ⎫
   Gayten-Thorpe.   ⎬ NORFOLK.
Hen. Meriton, Rector of *Oxborow.*   ⎪
Lancaster Topcliffe, L. B. sometimes ⎪
Sen. Fell. of *Gon.* & *Caius* Coll. *Cambr.* ⎭

LONDON,
Printed for *John Harris* at the *Harrow* in *Little-Britain.* MDCXCIX.

A Brief DISCOVERY of some of the Blasphemous and Seditious Principles and Practices of the People called Quakers.

GEO. FOX, the first Founder and great Apostle of this Sect, Gr. Myst. p. 209. saith against his Opponent thus; 'This Light that doth 'Enlighten every one that cometh into the World, 'which he calls Conscience, is not Conscience. And in p. 331. he further saith, 'The Light, which every 'one that cometh into the World, is Enlightened 'withal, is not Conscience, for the Light was before 'any thing was made, or Conscience named.

And G. F. Jun. in his Works, Reprinted 1665. p. 50. 'I the Light will fall upon you, and Grinde you to 'Powder. All—who will not own me the Light in you. 'And — I will make you know, That I the Light am the 'True Eternal God, which Created all things; and 'that by me, the Light, all things are upheld, and that 'there is not another besides me, that can Save.

In Geo. Fox's Book, styled, The Pearl found in England for the Scattered ones in Foreign Nations, the Royal Seed of God, and Heirs of Salvation, called Quakers, who are the Church of the Living God, per G. F. Printed 1658. where speaking in the Person of the Quakers Light, he hath these Passages, p. 15, 16. 'I'll break in 'Pieces: I'll make Nations like Dirt: I'll tread them 'into Mire: I'll make Religions, Professions and Teach-'ings—Gatherings on Heaps: Gatherings of Multi-'tudes; Gatherings which they call Churches: —I'll

The Quakers teach, That the Light within, by which they are guided, is not Conscience,

But the True Eternal God and Christ.

A 2   'make

' make Mire of them : I'll make Mortar : I'll make Dirt
' of them. The wrath of the Lamb is Rifen upon all
' Apoftates ; who are gathered in the Apoftacy. Apo-
' ftatized from the Prophets Life ; the Apoftles Life ;
' the Life of the Lamb : The Lamb is Rifen : The Scep-
' ter is gone out: The Throne is Set :——You fhall be
' Shaken——ye Diviners, ye Dreamers, ye Notionifts,
' ——I'll Whirl you under Hailftones, Viols, Plagues,
' Thunders, Woes, Judgments are come amongft you ;
' upon your Heads all Nations :——The pure Life of
' God is Rifen : ——From the Life of my Apoftles ; of
' my Prophets, have ye been all Scattered, and Apofta-
' tized :——But the Rod (*i.e.* our Light) is over you ;
' which muft Rule all Nations : Trumpets founding ;
' and Sounded, the Juft will Rule : The Lamb will have
' the Victory : Woes, Woes, and Miferies, are out-go-
' ing upon all the Heads of the Wicked.——What our
' Hands have handled ; and what our Eyes have feen ;
' what was from the Beginning, the Word of Life ; this
' Declare we unto you.

Again, G. *Fox* in his Book ftiled, *The Teachers of the
World unvailed*, &c. who in *p.* 27. thus faith : ' I am
' the Light of the World, H I M by whom the World
' was made : If you love the Light with which you
' are Enlightened withal, you love Chrift, who faith,
· Learn of me : But if you hate that Light, there is
' your Condemnation : From H I M who is one with
' the Truth in every Man ; Who of the Lord W A S
' moved T H I S to W R I T E :——Whofe Name of
' the World is called *Geo. Fox.*

And to this another of their Eminent Teachers,
one of their Prophets, fay *Amen*, in his Book, *The Quakers Challenge*, &c. Printed 1668. in thefe Words, *p.* 6.
' Stand up *Muggleton* the Sorcerer, whofe Mouth is
' full of Curfing, Lies, and Blafphemy ; who calls thy
' laft

' laſt Book, A Looking-Glaſs for *G EO. FO X*, whoſe
' Name thou art not worthy to take into thy Mouth,
' who is a P R O P H E T indeed, and hath been Faith-
' ful in the Lord's Buſineſs from the beginning. It was
' laid of Chriſt, That he was in the World, and the
' World was made by him, and the World knew him
' not : S O it may be ſaid of T H I S true Prophet
' [*Gen. Fox*] whom *John* ſaid he was not : But thou
' wilt feel this Prophet [*G. Fox*] one Day as heavy
' as a Milſtone upon thee : And although the World
' knows him not, yet he is known. And *pag.* 2, 3.
' Come Proteſtants, Presbyters, Independents and Bap-
' tiſts ; the Quakers denies you all. ――The Quakers
' are in the Truth, and none but they, *&c.* Now from
ſuch Proteſtans as theſe, *Good Lord deliver us* ; not-
withſtanding their now Wording the Matter otherwiſe,
whilſt they mean the ſame thing ; and their Principles
the ſame that ever they were, as they themſelves ſay,
and that in every part ; of which here is but a Spe-
cimen.

  Edward Burroughs (ſtiled a Son of Thunder, and
Conſolation ; a true Prophet, and faithful Servant of
God, in his Works Reprinted 1672.) *p.* 149. has an
Anſwer to this Queſtion ; ' Is that very Man, with that
' very Body within you, Yea or Nay ? He ſaith, ' The
' very Chriſt of God is within us, we dare not deny
' him.

  G. F. *Great Myſt. p.* 91. ' They ſhall ſee the Biſhop
' of their Souls, Chriſt the Power of God, which is Im-
' mortal, brings the Immortal Soul into the Immortal
' God. Chriſt their Sanctification, who ſanctifies their
' Spirits and Bodies, and brings the Soul up into God,
'from whence it came,whereby they came to be one Soul.
' *p.* 100. And is not that which came out from God,
' which God hath in his Hand (*ſpeaking of the Soul*)

                    ' taken

2.
That they are one Soul with God.

'taken up into God again, which Chrift the power of
'God is Bifhop of, is not this of God's Being?

That their Soul is part of God. *Idem*, p. 273. The Prieft fays, 'That it is Horrid
'Blafphemy, to fay the Soul is part of God. *G. F.* An-
fwers, 'It is not Horrid Blafphemy to fay the Soul is
'a part of God, for it came out of him, and that which
'came out of him, is of him, and rejoiceth in him.
And p. 100. 'God who hath all Souls in his Hand;
'and is not this that cometh out from God, which is
'in God's Hand, part of God?

That it is Infinite in it felf, without Beginning or Ending. *Pag.* 90. 'Is not the Soul, without beginning, co-
'ming from God——And Chrift the power of God,
'the Bifhop of the Soul, which brings it up into God,
'which came out from him, Hath this a Beginning or
'Ending? And is not this infinite in it felf, and more
'than all the World?

They make themfelves Equal with God. *G. F. Saul's Errand to Damafcus,* Printed 1654. p. 8.
'He that hath the fame Spirit, that raifed up Jefus Chrift,
'is Equal with God.

Fr. Howgil's Works, Printed 1676. p. 232. faith to
his Opponent; 'The firft thing that thy dark mind
'ftumbleth at, is, that fome have faid, That they that
'have the Spirit of God, are Equal with God: *Whereunto he Replies,* 'He that is joined to the Lord is one
'Spirit, there is Unity, and the Unity ftands in Equa-
'lity it felf. When the Son is revealed and fpeaks,
'the Father fpeaks in him, and dwells in him, and he
'in the Fath.r, in that which is Equal, in Equality it
'felf, there is Equality in Nature, tho' not in Stature.

3.
That they Affert themfelves to be Infallible. *G. F. Gr. Myft.* p. 107. He faith (*fpeaking of the
Prieft*) 'The Holieft Man that is, is not able to give
'an Infallible Character of another Man. *To which he
Anfwers:* 'Haft not thou in this difcovered thy felf
'to be no Minifter of Chrift, or of the Spirit, who
'cannot give an Infallible Character of another Man?
'How

'How canſt thou Miniſter to his Condition ? *Pag. 96.*
'And thou not being Infallible, thou art not in the
'Spirit, and ſo art not a Miniſter of Chriſt, and art not
'able to judge of Powers that is not Infallible , nor Ma-
'giſtrates, nor Kingdoms, nor Churches. *Pag.* 33. 'And
'are they Miniſters of Chriſt, that are Fallible ?
    Edw. Burr. p. 862. ' Such (i. e. *Hereticks*) are Infal-
'libly known, and diſcerned, by the Spirit of God, in
'the True Church of Chriſt, and by every Member of
'the ſame.

    Geo. F. Gr. Myſt. p. 282. Whereas Mr. *Cawdry* ſaid, *That they are*
'Surely they cannot be Perfect here, or hereafter, in Perfect *as* God.
'Equality, but only in Quality. *Fox* Anſwers, ' Chriſt
'makes no diſtinction in his Words, but ſaith, *Be ye*
'*Perfect, even as your Heavenly Father is* : And as he is,
'ſo are we : And that which is Perfect, as he is Perfect,
'is in Equality with the ſame thing ; which is of God,
'and from God.

    *G. F. Myſt. p.*101. ſaith, ' It is the Doctrine of Devils, *That they are*
'that Preacheth, That Men ſhall have Sin, and be in a without Sin.
'WARFARE, ſo long as they be on Earth. *Pag.* 231.
'All who come to Chriſt the Second *Adam*, they come
'to Perfection ; and all who attain to him, they at-
'tain to Perfection in the Life of God, out of the Firſt
'*Adam. Pag.* 271. ' For who are Sanctified, have per-
'fect Unity, perfect Knowledge, perfect Holineſs.

    And *William Penn*, in his *Truth Exalted*, Reprinted
1671. *p.* 9. laughs at the Church of *England*-Men, for
Confeſſing themſelves Sinners, or Praying to God for
Mercy : ——' Alas, poor Souls ! *(ſaith he)* are not
'you at, *Have Mercy upon us, miſerable Sinners* ; *there is*
'*no Health in us*, from Seven to Seventy.

    And *Edw. Burr. p.* 33. ſaith, ' That God doth not
'accept any, where there is any Failing : All who do
'not fulfil the Law, and Anſwer every Demand of Ju-
'ſtice. In

That they have Immediate Revelation, Equal with the Prophets and Apostles.

In *Truth defending the Quakers*, written from the Spirit of Truth, in *George Whitehead* and *George Fox* Junior, Printed 1659. *p.* 7. The Question being put, ' Whether the Quakers did efteem their Speakings, to ' be of as great Authority, as any Chapter in the Bible ? 'Tis Anfwer'd, ' That which is fpoken from the Spi- ' rit of Truth in any, is of as great Authority as the ' Scriptures and Chapters are, and GREATER.

G. F. Gr. Myft. p. 242. tells us, that the Prieft faith, ' That the Apoftles were Eye-Witnefles, and under- ' ftood by Immediate Revelation from God, Infpired ' with the Gift of the Spirit, more than any Man could ' hope for fince : And faith, 'They do not pretend ' any fuch Gift, nor depend upon fuch any Immediate; ' Miraculous Revelation from Heaven. To which *G.F.* anfwers, ' Then all may fee now in this, what ye have ' received, that hath been from Man, which is not ' from Heaven immediate, nor the Gifts of the Spirit, ' nor received the Gofpel, by the fame means the Apo- ' ftles did, who were not the Eye-Witnefles, as the ' Apoftles were : Neither have ye attained to the fame ' Knowledge and Underftanding, as the Apoftles did, ' nor received it from Heaven. Now let all People ' queftion, Whether it is the fame Gofpel, which is not ' received from Heaven, nor Immediately, nor by Re- ' velation, for the Gofpel is Immediate, which is the ' Power of God, *Rom.* 1. They (i. e. *Quakers*) are ' in the fame Power, Underftanding, Knowledge, and ' Immediate Revelation from Heaven, that the *Apoftles* ' were in.

Geo. Fox further tells us, *p.* 213. that the Prieft fays, ' Thou doft not fpeak in that Degree of the Holy ' Ghoft, as the Prophets and Apoftles did, that fpoke ' forth Scriptures : *To which he Anfwers,* ' Then thou ' muft take heed of Exalting thy felf above thy mea-
' fure,

' fure, for thou canft not know Scripture, but by the fame
' Degree of the Spirit, the Prophets and Apoftles had.

5.
They Vilifie and
Speak Contemp-
tuoufly of the
Scriptures.

    News coming up out of the North, written from the Mouth
of the Lord, from one who is Naked, and ftands Naked
before the Lord, Cloathed with Righteoufnefs, whofe Name is
not known in the World, rifen up out of the North, which
was Prophefied of, but now it is fulfilled, C A L L E D G. F.
Printed 1655. p. 14. ' Your Original is Carnal, Hebrew,
' Greek and Latin, and your Word is Carnal the Letter,
' and the Light is Carnal the Letter: -----Their Original
' is but Duft, which is but the Letter, which is Death:
'.-----And their G O S P E L I S B U T D U S T, M A I-
' T H E W, M A R K, L U K E, and J O H N, which is
' the Letter.

    Tho. Lawfon in his Brief Difcovery of a Threefold Eftate
of Antichrift, Printed 1653. written from the Spirit of the
Lord, p. 9. Calls the Minifters, ' Babylon's Merchants, fel-
' ling Beaftly Wares, for a large Price,-----the LETTER,
' which is DUST and DEATH.

    Saul's Errand to Damafcus, Printed 1654. p. 7. It was
Objected to the Quakers, that they had faid, Whoever
took a place of Scripture, and made a Sermon of it, or
from it, was a Conjurer, and his Preaching was Conjuration. To which G. Fox Anfwered, ' All that do Study
' to Raife a Living Thing out of a Dead, to Raife the
' Spirit out of the Letter, are Conjurers, and draw Points
' and Reafons, and fo do fpeak a Divination of their
' own Brain, they are Conjurers and Diviners, and their
' Teaching is from Conjuration, which is not Spoken
' from the Mouth of the Lord.

    Truths Defence, given forth by the Light and Power of
God, appearing in G. Fox and Rich. Hubberthorn, Printed 1653. p. 101. It is DANGEROUS to read (viz. the
the Scriptures) which the Prophets, Chrift, and the Apoftles
fpoke forth freely. And p. 2. fpeaking of fome of their
Queries, which were lookt upon as frivolous, and fhould
have been Burnt: They faid, You might as well have Con-

B   demned

demned the SCRIPTURES to the FIRE. And *p.* 104.
they give their reason why, faying, *Our giving forth Papers or Printed Books, is from the Immediate Eternal Spirit of God.*

Edw. Burr. p. 47. of his Works, having this Charged upon him, as the Principle of the Quakers, that Saints were not to do Duties, by, or from a Command without, but from a Command within ; and that the word *Command* in Scripture, was not a Command to them, till they had a Word within them : He Anfwers, 'That is no
' Command from God to me, what he Commands to ano-
' ther ; neither did any of the Saints which we' read of
' in Scripture, act by the Command, which was to ano-
' ther, not having the Command to themfelves. ——And
' thou, or any other, who goeft to Duty, as you call it,
' by imitation from the Letter without, which was a Com-
' mand to others, in your own Wills and Time, your
' Sacrifice is not Accepted, but is Abomination to the
' Lord ; for you go without the moving of the Spirit,
' in your own Wills and Strength, which God Hates, and
' which his Wrath is upon.

Agreeable to which, *William Penn* in his *Quakerifm a new Nick Name,* &c. Printed 1673. *p.* 71, 72. Afferts,
' No Command in the Scripture, is any further Obliging
' upon any Man, than as he finds a Conviction upon his
' Confcience ; otherwife, Men fhould be ingaged with-
' out, if not againft, Conviction ; a thing unreafonable
' in a Man : ——So that Conviction can only Oblige
' to Obedience : And when any Man is Convinced, That
' what was Commanded another, is Required of him, then,
' and not till then, he is rightly Authorized to perform
' it.

And alfo affert, that the Scriptures are No Rule.

A Shield of the Truth, written from the Spirit of the Lord, by Jam. Parnell, Printed 1655. *p.* 11. 'He that faith, the
' Letter is the Rule, and Guide of the People of God, is
' Without, feeding upon the Husk, and is Ignorant of
' the True Light.

Edw.

Edw. Bur. p. 515. tells us, ' That the Scriptures, are
' not the Rule and Guide of Faith and Life, unto the
' Saints, but the Spirit of God, that gave forth the Scrip-
' tures.

And further, in a Teftimony from the Brethren, met
together at *London*, in the Third Month, 1666. to be
Communicated to the faithful Friends and Elders, in
the Countries, by them to be read in their feveral Meetings, and kept as a Teftimony among them, Signed by
Rich. Farnfworth, Alex. Parker, George Whitehead, and
Eight more ; who, by the Operation of the Spirit of
Truth, being brought into a Serious Confideration of
this prefent State of the Church of God, *&c.* Declare in
the Third Section, ' If any Difference arife in the Church,
' or amongft them, that Profefs themfelves Members
' thereof, we do Declare and Teftifie, That the Church,
' with the Spirit of the Lord Jefus Chrift, have Power
' (without the Affent of fuch as Diffent from their Do-
' ctrines and Practices) to Hear and Determine the
' fame: If any pretend to be of us, and, in Cafe of Con-
' troverfie, will not admit to be Tried by the Church of
' Chrift Jefus, nor fubmit to the Judgment given by the
' Spirit of Truth, in the Elders and Members of the fame,
' but kick againft their Judgment, as only the Judgment
' of Man, it being Manifefted according to Truth, and
' Confiftent with the Doctrine of *fuch Good Antient*
' *Friends*, as have been, and are Sound in the Faith,
' agreeable to the *Witnefs of God in his People*, then we
' do Teftifie in the *Name of the Lord* (if that Judgment
' fo given be Rifen againft, and Denied by the Party
' Condemned,) then he or fhe ought to be Rejected, as
' having Erred from the Truth ; and perfifting therein
' Prefumptuoufly, are joined in one with Heathens and
' Infidels.

And purfuant to which, Mr. *Keith* was Proceeded
againft, in *Penfylvania*, as guilty of Herefie ; not from
the Scriptures, as he defired, but from Friends. Books ;
and

and was told by *Sam. Jennings*, (a great Teacher, and Juftice of Peace there) in the Publick Meeting : 'We 'are not to prove it from Scripture, but from Friends 'Books ; *for the Queftion between us and G. K. is not, who* 'is *the beft Chriftian, but the beft Quaker ?* And accordingly they produced, inftead of Scripture, a Citation out of *William Penn*'s Chriftian Quaker, to prove him a Heretick.   *See* G. K's *Herefie and Hatred*, Printed at *Philadelphia*, 1693.

6.
They affert that Chrift's Flefh is a Figure.
Saul's Errand to Damafcus, p. 14. The Queftion was put to *Geo. Fox*, Whether Chrift in the Flefh be a Figure or not ; and if a Figure, How, and in What ? To which he Anfwers, *Chrift is the Subftance of all Figures, and his Flefh is a Figure.*   And in *Truth defending the Quakers*, by G. *Whitehead*, &c. p. 20. It is faid exprefly, *That Chrift's coming in the Flefh, is but a Figure.*

And that Chrift was Crucified within us, and any other was Anti-Chrift.
G. F. *Gr. Myft.* p. 206. ' The Apoftles Preached Chrift 'that was Crucified within, and not another ; him that 'was Raifed up from the Dead, was Rifen that Lord Je-'fus Chrift within : ——It was he that was manifeft in 'the Saints, that was, and is not another.   FOR THE 'OTHER IS THE ANTI-CHRIST. ——Now 'I fay, if there be any other Chrift, but HE THAT 'WAS CRUCIFIED WITHIN, HE IS THE FALSE 'CHRIST. ——And he that hath not this Chrift, that 'was Rifen and Crucified, within, is a Reprobate ; the 'Devils and Reprobates may make a talk of him with-'out.

7.
They Vilifie and Deny the Sacraments, viz. Baptifm by Water, and the Lord's Supper by Bread and Wine.
G. F. *News coming up,* &c. *p.* 14. ' Your Baptifm is 'Carnal——And their Sacrament, as they call it, is Car-'nal ——And their Communion is Carnal ; a little Bread 'and Wine.   And *p.* 34. 'A Voice and a Word, to all 'you Deceivers, who deceive the People ; and Blafphe-'mers, who utter forth your Blafphemy, and Hypocrifie ; 'that tell People of a Sacrament, and tell them it is the 'Ordinance of God ; Blufh, Blufh and Tremble before 'the Almighty, for Dreadful is he that will pour forth his 'Vengeance upon you.   *Smith's*

Smith's *Primer*, Printed 1668. *p.* 6. ' I would know
' Father *(faith the Child)* how it is concerning thofe
' things called Ordinances, as Baptifm, and Bread, and
' Wine, which are much ufed in their Worfhip? *The*
' *Father Anfwers* : Why Child, as to thofe things, they
' arofe from the Pope's Invention, who hath had Power
' in the Night of Apoftacy: And hath fet up his Devices,
' which are yet continued in *England*, tho' he feeming'y
' is denied : And the whole practice of thofe things, as
' they ufe them, had their INSTITUTION BY THE
' POPE, and were never fo Ordain'd of Chrift.

William Penn's Reafon againft Railing, Printed 1673.
p. 108, 109. ' I affirm, by that one Scripture (*Hebr.* 9.
' 10.) that Circumcifion is as much in force as Wa-
' ter-Baptifm ; and the Pafchal-Lamb, as Bread and
' Wine ; they were both Shadows, and both Elementary,
' and Perifhable : ——For a Continuance of them had
' been a Judaizing of the Spiritual Evangelical Worfhip,
' the Gofpel would have been a State of Figures, Types,
' and Shadows. ——And we can Teftifie, from the fame
' Spirit, by which *Paul* renounced Circumcifion, that they
' are to be rejected, as not now required : Neither have
' they, fince the Falfe Church Efpoufed and Exalted them,
' ever been taken up afrefh by God's Command, or in
' the Leadings of his Eternal Spirit ; and the Lord will
' appear, to Gather a People out of them, but never to
' Eftablifh or Keep People in them : No, they Served
' their time, and now the Falfe Church has got them ;
' yea, and the Whore has made Merchandize with them,
' and under fuch Hiftorical, Shadowy, and Figurative
' Chriftianity, has fhe managed her Myftery of Iniquity,
' unto the beguiling of Thoufands.

G. F. *News coming up*, &c. *p.* 4. ' Your Baptifm and
' Sacraments, as you call it, and all your Ordinances, and
' Churches, and Teachings, it is *Cain's* Sacrifice. *p.* 14.
One Quaker writes to another in a bemoaning Letter,
called, *The Spirit of the Hat*, Printed 1673. *p.* 12. Com-
plaining

8.
They allow No
*Liberty to any
who differ from
them.*

plaining of *Geo. Fox*'s not allowing any Liberty ; He speaketh thus : ' My Friend, Obferve what difference is ' there in thefe things, between *G. F.* and the Papifts ? ' The one faith, No Liberty out of the Church ; the other, ' No Liber y out of the Power : Saith the Papift, What ! ' Liberty to the Sectary ? No. What ! Liber y to the He-' retick ? No. And *G. F.* faith : What ! Liberty to the ' Presbyter ? No. What ! Liberty to the Independent ? ' No. What ! Liberty to the Baptift ? No. Liberty ' *(faith he)* is in the Truth : The difference lies only ' here, the one has greater Power to Compel than the ' other.

William Penn in his *Brief Examination, and State of Liberty Spiritual,* Printed 1681. *p.* 3. where the Queftion is : *Muft I Conform to things, whether I can receive them or no ? Ought I not to be left to the Grace and Spirit of God in my own Heart ?* To the firft he fays, *Nay* ; to the laft, *Yea.* But he bids them Confider, *Whether it is from their Weaknefs or Carelefnefs* ; telling them, *It is a dangerous Principle, and pernicious to True Religion : Nay, it is the Root of* Ranterifm, *to Affert, That nothing is a Duty Incumbent upon thee, but what thou art perfwaded is thy Duty.* And in *p.* 11. *I affirm from the Underftanding I have received of God, not only that the Enemy is at Work, to fcatter the Minds of Friends, by that loofe Plea* ; *What haft thou to do with me, leave me to my Freedom, and to the Grace of God in my felf.* But this Propofition, as now Underftood and Alledged, is a Deviation from, and a Pervertion of, the Ancient Principle of Truth, *&c.*

And in *p.* 12. ' Some under pretence of Crying down 'MAN, FORMS, AND PRESCRIPTIONS, ' are Crying down the Heavenly Man Chrift Jefus, his ' bleffed Order and Government, which he hath brought ' forth by his own Revelation and Power, through his ' Faithful Witneffes. *Which Revelation, p.* 13. *was concerning Men and Womens Meetings :* ' Wherefore I warn ' all, (faith *Penn*) that they have a Care, how they give 'way,

(15)

' way, to the Outcry of fome, falfly intituled Liberty of
' Confcience, againft Impofitions, &c. Nor is it the leaft
' Evil this Spirit of Strife is Guilty of, that uleth the words
' Liberty of Confcience, and Impofitions againft the Bre-
' thren, in the fame manner, as our Suffering Friends have
' been accuftomed, to intend them againft the Perfecu-
' ting PRIESTS AND POWERS of the Earth.   9.

Edw. Bnr. his Works, *p.* 244. ' The Lord is rifen to *They Declare themfelves a-*
'Overturn, to Overturn, Kings and Princes, Govern- *gainft* Kingly
' ments and Laws: ———And he will Change Times, and *Government*
' Laws, and Governments; and there fhall be no King
' Ruling, but Jefus; nor no Government of Force, but
' the Government of the Lamb ; nor no Law of Effect,
' but the Law of God : All that which is otherwife, fha'll
' be ground to Powder. And *p.* 507. he faith further :
' But as for this People (i. e. *Quakers*) they are Raifed
' of the Lord, and Eftablifhed by him, E V E N C O N-
'T R A R Y T O A L L M E N, and they have given
' their Power only to God; and they cannot give their
' Power to A N Y M O R T A L M E N, to ftand or
' fall by any O U T W A R D A U T H O R I T Y, and
' to that they cannot feek, but to the Lord alone.

And *G. F.* in his *Gr. Myft. p.* 31. faith, ' That the
' Quakers are in the Power of God, and in the Autho-
' rity of the Lamb, above all Houfes, and into Houfes
' Creep not, BUT ARE UPON THE THRONE.

And in *Truth defending the Quakers,* Printed 1659.
p. 9, 10. *Geo. Whitehead* and *G. F.* Junior, being asked,
*Whether they did not fay, That the Magiftrate who made
Acts of Parliament, and doth not receive them from God,
as* Mofes; *doth act contrary to the Law of God.* They Anfwered, *The Magiftrate that is fent of God, he receives the
Law from the Mouth of God; and he is the Prophet whom*
Mofes *fpake of,* Deut. 18. 18. And rebukes them for
thinking, Men fhould make Acts, and not receive them
from God. They fay again, *The Man-Child appears, who
muft Rule the Nations with a Rod of Iron.*

G. Fox

(16)

G. Fox in his Book, *Several Papers given forth*, &c. to Presbyterians, *&c.* juft before the Reftoration, Writ *Anno* 1659. and Printed the beginning of 1660. he hath thefe Paffages : ' Friends ; to all you that defire an Earth-'ly King in *England*, &c. whether Presbyterians, or o-' thers : ——Did the Elders of Old, in the Days of Chrift, ' or the Apoftles, Cry up any King but Chrift ; to have ' any King to Rule over them but Chrift : And doth not ' the Priefts and Presbyterians Cry for an Earthly King, ' and will have Cæfar ? ——And do they not in this ' C R U C I F Y Jefus ? ——Are not all thefe Elders, that ' will Doat fo much of an Earthly King, TRAYTORS ' againft Chrift ? ——Do you read that there were any ' Kings fince the Days of the Apoftles, but among the ' A P O S T A T E C H R I S T I A N S ? ——For Chrift is ' King alone : ——I fay, That is the Falfe Church, that ' doth not live——upon the Head of the Kings : ----They ' that be True Elders,——never go about to Set Up an ' Earthly King over them to Rule : ——*Herod* the King ' was Mad at the Child Jefus ; ——there is the Fruit of ' Earthly Kings : ——And hath not this been Witneffed ' in *England* ? &c. Ignorant and Foolifh People, that ' would have a King : And what work *Jofhua* made ' with the Kings ; how he brought them out of the Cave, A F I T P L A C E F O R T H E M : ——And all thefe ' Novices Chriftians ; that are Crying up Earthly Kings : ' ——And we know that thefe Kings are the S P I R I-' T U A L E G Y P T I A N S got up fince the Days of ' the Apoftles, *&c.* Thus much briefly touching their Ancient Anti-Monarchical Principles ; and they are the fame ftill, and have not Deviated in any one Point, only *G. Whitehead* tells us, they may fee Caufe otherwife to Word the Matter, *&c.*

Againft the Houfe of Lords ' Oh ! What fincerity was once in the Nation, *fays* ' *G. F. to the Council of Officers*, 1659. *p.* 7. What a Dirty ' Nafty thing it would have been, to have heard talk ' of a Houfe of Lords amongft them.

Again,

Again, G. F. to the Parliament of the Commonwealth
of *England*, &c. *p.* 8. faith, *viz.* ' Let all Abby-Lands,
' Gleab-Lands, that's given to the Priests, be given to the
' Poor : And let all the great Houfes, Abbies, Steeple-
' Houfes, and *Whitehall*, be for Alms-Houfes, for all the
' Blind and Lame to be there, *&c.* And they are of the
fame Principles ftill ; they tell you fo, as in the Conclu-
fion you will fee it proved from their late Writings.

Again, in their Book ftiled, *Thefe feveral Papers fent to
the Parliament, the Twentieth of the Fifth Month,* 1659.
Infcrib'd by above Seven Thoufand Quakers, there is
thefe Paffages, *p.* 63. ' Sell all the Gleab-Lands ; and the
· Bells, except One in a Town, or Two in a City, to give
' Notice of Fire : And all the late King's Parks, and his
' Rents, and the Abbies ; and deny your felves of his
' [*i. e.* King's] Parks, Houfes, and Rents : So let them
' be fold ; and the Colledges fold : ——For we Declare
' with our Hands, and with our Lives and Eftates, againft
' the Miniftry that take Tythes ; and the Setters of them
' up ; and the firft Authors of them ; and the Laws that
' Upholds them, *&c.* And they are the fame ftill, they
have not Deviated from their Old Principles, (as they
themfelves fay) only they think it Prudent otherwife to
word the Matter ; as afterwards you'l hear.

Geo. Fox Junior, in his Works, Reprinted 1665. *p.* 87, And Houfe of
88. Intitles his Epiftle, ' *A few Plain Words, to be Confider-* Commons.
' *ed by thofe of the Army, or others, that would have a Par-*
' *liament, Chofen by the Voices of the People,* &c. Wheren is
' fhewed unto them, according to the Scriptures of Truth,
' That a Parliament fo Chofen, are not like to govern,
' for God, or the good of his People : Confider thefe
' things (*fays he*) which I Declare unto you, which in
' waiting upon the Lord, he by his Spirit of Wifdom
' and Underftanding, Opened in me, concerning the
' Chufing of Parliments, by the Voices of the People.
And *p.* 89. he fays, ' You are not like to fee your defires
' fulfilled, by a Parliament Chofen by the Voices of the
D   ' People :

(18)

‘ People : —Now if you believe thefe Scriptures, *Joh.* 15.
‘ 19. *Math.* 7. 13. *Rom.* 9. 27. then may you fee, *That a*
‘ *Parliament that is Chofen by moft Voices, are not like to act*
‘ *for God and the good of his People.* And *p.* 91. ‘ And
‘ likewife, the *Chufing of Parliament Men, according to the*
‘ *Cuftom of* England, which is called its Birth-right, *ftands*
‘ *in refpect of Perfons, and not in Equality ;* for the Rich,
‘ Covetous, Oppreffing Men, who Opprefs the Poor,
‘ they have the only Power to Chufe Law-makers ; and
‘ they will Chufe, to be fure, fuch as will uphold them
‘ in their Oppreffion. And *p.* 92, 93. And we fee, the
‘ People have been in great B'indnefs, in contending for
‘ *Parliaments fo Chofen. Pag.* 149. Again, it is God's pro-
‘ per right to give Laws unto Man. —Now in this par-
‘ ticular alfo, Man have fet himfelf in the Seat of God ;
‘ and fo have Difhonoured the one Law-giver, by fetting
‘ up many Law-givers. *Pag.* 150. Now Mark and
‘ Confider thefe things, feeing that the Righteous are
‘ fewer in Number, than the Unrighteous, and that the
‘ Law-makers are Chofen by the moft Voices, and that
‘ of the Richeft People outwardly, how are the Righte-
‘ ous like to be preferved, in outward Freedom, by the
‘ Laws that are fo made ? *Pag.* 159. And I muft deal
‘ plainly with you *(faith he)* in the fight of God, who
‘ hath made me a *PROPHET TO THIS NA-*
‘ *TION.*

Again, *Edw. Burroughs* in his Works, *p.* 522. — ‘ A
‘ Running to the Powers of the Earth : What have you
‘ Minifters loft the Lord to be your Strength, that you
‘ muft flee for help to Men ? Muft they make Laws to
‘ Eftablifh you, and Set you Up ? Is not this the Whore
‘ that Rode upon the Beaft, and that the Beaft Carried:
Again, *p.* 524. to the Parliament thus, *viz.* ‘ You do but
‘ caufe people to drink of the Whores Cup ; and you
‘ are but them (*i. e.* Beaft) which Carry the Whore,
‘ *viz.* the Falfe Church : And this is plain dealing to tell
‘ you the Truth ; for we are Gathered up into the Life
‘ which

' which the Holy Men of God Lived in, and are fallen
' from the World, and its Ways, and Nature : *p.* 50. For
' even the *F A T H E R* bears Witnefs of us ; and therefore
' our Witnefs is True.

 News coming up, &c. *Geo. Fox, p.* 18. ' Dreadful is the *Againfl* Judges,
' Lord and Powerful, who is coming in his Power, to Juftices, and Conftables.
' Execute true Judgment, upon all you Judges ; and to
' Change all your Laws, ye Kings ; and all you Rulers
' muft down and ceafe : —And all you Underling-Of-
' ficers, which have been as the Arms of this great Tree,
' which the Fowls have lodged under : —All your Bran-
' ches muft be C U T down, for you have been all the
' Fruitlefs Branches, grown on the Fruitlefs Tree. *Pag.*
' 20. Sing all ye Saints, and Rejoice, Clap your Hands,
' and be Glad, for the Lord Jehovah will Reign, and
' the Government fhall be taken from you pretended
' *Rulers, Judges* and *Juftices, Lawyers* and *Conftables,* all
' this Tree muft be Cut down ; and Jefus Chrift (in us)
' will Rule alone : So you muft be Cut down with the
' fame Power, *p.* 19. that Cut down the *King that Reign-*
' *ed over the Nation.*

 And in *Edw. Bur.* Works, Printed 1659. and Reprint-
ed in 1672. and Recommended by the fame *Geo. Fox,*
Fran. Howgil, Geo. Whitehead, Jof. Coale, &c. *p.* 501. he
faith, ' We ftand Witneffes againft *Parliaments, Councils,*
' *Judges, Juftices,* who *Make* or *Execute* Laws in their
' Will, over the Confciences of Men, or Punifh for Con-
' fcience fake : And to fuch Laws, Cuftoms, Courts, or
' Arbitrary Ufurped Dominion, W E cannot yield O U R
' Obedience, &c.

 Again, *Geo. Fox* to the Parliament of the Common- *Againft* Law-
' Wealth of *England,* &c. faith, *p.* 5. ' Away with *Capmen,* yers.
' and *Coifmen,* as they are called ; away with all thofe
' *Counfellers,* that will not tell Men the Law without Ten
' Shillings, Twenty Shillings, or Thirty Shillings : —And
' away with thofe Lawyers, Twenty Shillings Counfellers,
' Thirty Shillings Serjeants, Ten-Groats Attorneys.
             Again,

(20)

Againſt Lords of Manours.
Again, p. 8. *ibid.* 'Let all thoſe Fines that belong to
' *Lords of Manours*, be given to Poor People, for *Lords*
' have enough.

16.
Which Govern-ment, that they might not Sup-port, they De-clare againſt the Uſe of the Carnal Wea-pon, in 1660.
A Declaration from the People of God (called Quakers)
againſt all Plotters *and* Fighters, *&c.* preſented to King
Charles II. 1660. ' All Bloody Principles and Practices,
' We, as to our own Particulars, do utterly Deny, with
' all outward *WARS*, and Strife, and Fightings, with
' outward *WEAPONS*, for any end, or under any
' pretence whatſoever. And this is our Teſtimony, to
' the whole World : And we do certainly Know, and
' ſo Teſtifie to the World, that the Spirit of Chriſt, which
' leads us into all Truth, will never move us to Fight
' and *WAR* againſt any Man with *outward Weapons*,
' either for the Kingdom of Chriſt, nor for the Kingdom
' of this World, *&c.* Subſcribed by *Geo. Fox, Sam. Fiſher,*
' and many more.

Altho' none be-fore, ſo much for it as they.
The aforeſaid *Sam. Fiſher*, in his Works, Printed 1656.
and Reprinted 1679. and recommended to the World,
amongſt others, by *William Penn*, who tells us, *That theſe
things, came not to him by Fleſh and Blood, but by the Revelation of the Father of Lights.* And thus the ſaid *Sam.
Fiſher* ſpeaks, in a Meſſage from the Lord, to *O. Cromwell,*
and the Parliament of *England. p.* 19, 20. ' I will hold
' my Peace N O W no longer, ſaith the Lord, as con-
' cerning this Evil, which they ſo profanely Commit and
' Do Daily againſt my Choſen, but will utterly *SUB-
' VERT* and *OVERTURN* them, and bring the
' Kingdoms and Dominions, and the greatneſs of the
' Kingdom, under the whole Heaven, into the Hands
' of the *HOLY ONES* of the moſt High, and give
' unto my Son and his Saints, to Reign over all the Earth,
' and take all the Rule and Authority, and Power, that
' ſhall ſtand up againſt my Son in his Saints. ——And I
' will put my High Praiſes into their Mouth, and a Two
' Edged *SWORD* into their Hands, and they ſhall Exe-
' cute Vengeance upon the Heathen, and Puniſhments
' upon

(21)

'upon the People, and shall bind their Kings in Chains,
' and their Nobles in Fetters of Iron, and Execute upon
' them the Judgment, that is written, in my Eternal De-
' cree, and unchangeable Council, faith the Lord. *Given*
' *forth under my Hand, as the Lord himself gave it into my*
' *Heart to fee, and into my Mouth to speak in part, and un-*
' *to my Hand, thus at large to write it, this Twenty fifth Day*
' *of the fame Month (*viz. *the Seventh)* 1656.

Samuel Fisher.

Witnefs alfo the Quakers Declaration to *Oliver,* viz.
Oh! Oliver, *arife and come out,——for thou haft had Authority ; ftand to it : ——Nor let any other take thy Crown :
—And let thy Soldiers go forth with a free and willing Heart,
that thou mayeft* Rock Nations *as a Cradle. This is a Charge
to thee in the prefence of the Lord God.*

Alfo *Geo. Roffe* in his Book, Intituled, *The Righteoufnefs of God,*&c. Printed—p. 11. hath thefe words: ' To
' thee, *Oliv. Cromwell,* thus faith the Lord ; I have Cho-
' fen thee amongft the Thoufands of the Nations, to Exe-
' cute my Wrath upon mine Enemies, and gave them to
' thy Sword, with which I fought for the Zeal of my own
' Name, and gave thee the Enemies of my own Seed,
' to be a Curfe and a Reproach for ever, and made thee
' an Inftrument againft them ; and many have I Cut
' down by my Sword in thy Hand, that my wrath might
' be Executed upon them to the Uttermoft. Subfcribed

Geo. Roffe.

And *Geo. Fox,* in his Letter directed to the Council of
Officers of the Army, 1659, *&c.* Complains of many
Quakers Disbanded out of the Army (as well as Juftices
of the Peace) in thefe words, p. 5. ' And many Valiant
' Captains, Soldiers and Officers, have been put out of
' the Army (by Sea and Land) of whom it hath been
' faid among you, that they had rather have had one of
' them, than Seven Men, and could have turned one of
' them to Seven Men ; who, becaufe of their Faithful-

E ' nefs

' nefs to the Lord God, being Faithful towards him, it
' may be for faying Thou to a particular, and for Wear-
' ing their Hats, have been turned out from amongft
' them.

And may Re-
affume it a-
gain when they
fhall judge it
meet.

As appears to us, by a Declaration, wrote by *Edw.*
Bur. in the Name of all the Quakers, and Subfcribed by
feveral of the Principal Leaders of them, Printed 1659.
p. 8. They fpeak thus, ' We are Dreadful to the Wicked,
' and muft be their Fear, for we have Chofen the Son
' of God to be our King, and he hath Chofen us to be his
' People ; and he might Command Thoufands and Ten
' Thoufands of his Saints at this Day, to F I G H T in his
' Caufe ; he might lead them forth, and bring them in,
' and give them Victory over all their Enemies, and turn
' his Hand upon all their Perfecutors. But (*fay they*) *p.* 9.
' We cannot Y E T believe that he will make ufe of us
' I N T H A T W A Y, tho' it be his only Right to Rule
' in Nations, and O U R H E I R S H I P to poffefs the
' uttermoft parts of the Earth ; but for the P R E S E N T
' we are given up to Bear and Suffer.

I I.

*They have a Goverment within the
Government, Independent from it, and
Oppofite to it. Firft, their Monthly and
Quarterly Meetings, which are after the
manner of the* Juftices *Monthly Meetings,
and Quarterly Seffions in the Country,
which are Subordinate to the Yearly
Meeting ; which Yearly Meeting confifts
of Deputies from all the Counties in
England and Wales, as well as Agents
from beyond the Sea, and is their Su-
preme Affembly, which gives Laws to
the whole Body of the Quakers, where-
foever they are. And there they make
their Orders, for the Government of
their People : For Suppreffing of any
Books wrote againft them, and pafs
Cenfure upon Offenders : And there
alfo they take an account of their Fund,
which is raifed by an Order of this
Yearly Meeting, in all the Counties of
England and Wales, by way of Colle-
ftion : And the Money when Collected,*

Mr. *Bugg's Pilgrims Progrefs,*Chapters
7, 8, 9, 10, 11, give an Account of their
feveral Meetings, and of their *Fund, Ex-
chequer,* or *Common Bank.*

Mr. *Keith,* who has been a Quaker a-
bove Thirty Years, in his *Second Narra-
tive, p.* 5. fays, *I am not able to Print
Books as they* (Quakers) *can, they are
many, and have a* Common Stock ; *I am
but one.*

And in his Book, called, *The Pretended Yearly Meeting of the Quakers, their
Namelefs Bull of Excommunication, given
forth againft him,* &c. Printed 1695. *p.* 5.
fpeaks thus, ' To my certain Knowledge
' and Obfervation, I faw the Door of
' the Meeting (where that called the
' Yearly

'Yearly Meeting Sat) kept by Three or
'Four Perfons, that Refufed to let in
'fome that defired to come in, and yet
'were owned by them. And it is fuf-
'ficiently known, they who keep the
'Door, let in, or keep out, fuch as they
'think fit. But again, fuch as they let
'in, if they be not of the Miniftry, nor
'any of the Two Chofen out of every
'County, they are allowed only to be
'there as Standers By, and Spectators,
'but have no allowance to give any Judg-
'ment in the Cafe, which hath been a dif-
'couragement to fome honeft Friends, owned by the
'Yearly Meeting as Friends, from coming to the Meet-
'ing, being only permitted to be there as Cyphers. And
'yet further, it is fufficiently known, the way that they
'take, either by Perfwafions or Terrifications, to gain the
'Univerfal and Unanimous Confent, of them called Com-
'miffioners, or Chofen Members from every County ; as
'doth plainly appear, by the late moft Abfurd and In-
'folent Method, (more like the *Spanifh* Inquifition, than
'a Free Affembly of fincere Chriftians) they did take
'a Preacher, one of their Commiffioners, or Chofen Mem-
'bers, who having faid in Private, out of the Meeting,
'*He could fooner Die, or lofe his Right Hand, than Sign to*
'*a Paper Difowning G. K.* which coming to their Intel-
'ligence, that there was fuch a Perfon, but not knowing
'who he was, they were fo earneft to find him out, that
'they caufed to call over the Roll or Lift, of the Names
'of the Perfons fent from the refpective Counties, to find
'out this Perfon, asking them one by one to find him
'out. And the poor Man, not daring to Lye, owned he
'was the Perfon ; and being Terrified, left he fhould be
'feverely Proceeded againft by them, he came (with
'fome others, to be Witneffes of his Recantation,) and
'difowned to me, what he had formerly faid, tho' a few
'Hours

*is Tranfmitted to London, and lodg-
ed in the hands of* Six Feoffees, *who,
as to the Difpofal thereof, are to be Go-
verned, by the Second Day Meeting, held
on every* Monday *throughout the Year ;
which Money is for divers ufes, viz.
Stipends for their Teachers :* Wages
for their Clerks : Attendants *upon the
Houfes of Parliament :* For Printing
and Difperfing *of their* Books *: For
the Maintenance of the Poor : For the
Relief of fuch as have fuffered for* Non-
payment of Tythes, *and the Breach of
other Laws ; and for feveral other
things, tending to the Propagating of
their Doctrines, and Supporting of their
Government.*

' Hours before, he profefs'd fo great a Concern and Ten-
' dernefs of Confcience towards me. This Paffage is fo
' Confiderable an Advance towards the Erecting the *Spa-*
' *nifh* Inquifition among the Quakers, that I hope fome
' will be awakened to take notice of it, and withftand
' it.

And tho' the King and Parliament, were fo Gracious,
as to include the Quakers, in the Act made *primo Guliel-*
mi & Mariæ, For Exempting Their Majefties Proteftant
Subjects, Diffenting from the Church of England, *from the*
Penalty of certain Laws, &c. wherein it is Expreffed, *That*
nothing herein contained, fhall be Conftrued to Exempt any
of the Perfons aforefaid from paying of Tythes, or other Pa-
rochial Duties, or any other Duties to the Church or Mini-
fter: Yet notwithftanding, the Quakers in their Yearly
Epiftle, fent forth from their Yearly Meeting, held in *Lon-*
don, the Fifth, Sixth, Seventh and Eighth Days of the
Fourth Month, 1693. to the Monthly and Quarterly
Meeting of Friends, in *England, Wales,* and elfewhere,
thought fit to Order, ' That all Due and Godly Care be
' taken *(as they word it)* againft the *Grand Oppreffion,*
' *and Anti-Chriftian Yoke of Tythes, that our Chriftian Te-*
' *ftimony* (fay they) *born and greatly Suffered for, be faith-*
fully Maintained againft them in all refpects, and againft
Steeple-Houfes, Rates or Lays.

And in the fore Cited Teftimony from the Brethren,
met together in the Third Month, 1666. they take Care
to Stifle and Supprefs (what they can) all Books wrote
againft them : Ordering thus ; ' That if any Man or Wo-
' man, which are out of the Unity, with the Body of the
' Friends, Print, or caufe to be Printed, or Publifhed in
' Writing, any thing which is not of Service for the
' Truth, but tends to the Scandalizing, and Reproaching
' of faithful Friends, or to beget or uphold Divifion and
' Faction, then we do Warn and Charge all Friends, that
' do love Truth, as they defire it may Profper, and be
' kept clear, to beware and take heed, of having any
' Hand

'Hand in Printing, Republishing, or Spreading such
'Books or Writings. And if at any time such Books be
'sent, to any of you that Sell Books in the Countrey, (af-
'ter that you, with the Advice of Good and Serious
'Friends, have Tried them, and find them Faulty) to
'send them back again, whence they came. And we fur-
'ther desire, from time to time, Faithful and Sound
'Friends, may have the View of such things, as are Printed
'upon Truth's Account (*as formerly it hath used to be*)
'before they go to the Press, that nothing but what is
'Sound and Savory, and that may answer the Witness of
'God, even in our Adversaries, may be exposed to Pub-
'lick View.

Which Meeting, is one of the most Ancient Meetings *They have also*
for Government, made up of Chosen Men amongst them, *a Six Weeks*
expert in the Laws and Customs of the Nation, well skil- *Meeting.*
led in the Courts of *London* and *Westminster*, and other
His Majesties Courts of Record, and such as understand
the way and manner of Soliciting the Parliament : And
to support them in all these things, they have the *Common
Bank* to assist them. *F. B. Pilg. Prog. p. 65. ch. 10.*

In their fore-cited Yearly Epistle from their Yearly *They have also*
Meeting, held 1693. they Ordered, 'That Friends, at all *a Register of
their Sufferings,
'their Monthly and Quarterly Meetings, should be re- (which have
'minded, to call for the Records of the Sufferings of been inflicted for
'Friends, to see that they be duly Gathered, truly En- the Laws,)
'tred and Kept, and accordingly sent up (to *London*) as thereby to ren-
'hath been often advised, both of what Tythes, &c. are der the Gover-
'pretended to be due, and for how long a time, and the time ment odious for
'when taken, and by and for whom: And what Goods Persecution, to
'are taken, and the Value thereof, as well of those not do threaten, in
'exceeding, as those exceeding the Sums or Quantities After-ages, to
'demanded (it being a Suffering, in both, for Truth's sake) publish the same,
'they being in these particulars, found Defective and Im- of the things,
'perfect in divers Countries, which is an Obstruction and matters of
'to the General Record of Friends Sufferings. And there- gotten.
'fore the Monthly and Quarterly Meetings are advised

F   ' to

' to take more Care for the future, that all Friends Suffer-
' ings for the Truth's fake, may be brought up *as Full and*
' *Compleat in all respects as poffible may be.*
The Author of *Sathan Difrobed*, Printed 1698. *p.* 82.
Informs us, that in this Regifter, there are many Ground-
lefs, and many downright Falfhoods, which it is very fit
the World fhould know ; becaufe they take great Care
to fwe'l this Regifter, and have threatened to publifh it
to After-ages (when the Facts cannot be Difproved)
whereby they hope to make their Sufferings for the Truth
(as they call it) to exceed all the Ten Perfecutions, and
to be more Undeferved, than the Sufferings of Chrift himfelf, or of the Apoftles, as *Edw. Burr.* (their Second Pil-
ler next to *Geo. Fox*) exprefs'd in his Works, *p.* 273. ' The
' Sufferings of the People of God (*that is Quakers*) in
' this Age, is *greater Suffering, and more Unjuft, than in the*
' *Days of Chrift, or of the Apoftles, or in any time fince.*——
' What was done to Chrift or the Apoftles, was chiefly
' done by a Law, and in great part by the D U E Exe-
' cution of a Law, *&c.* And *p.* 85. faith he, It is here
worth Notice, That the firft Difference, betwixt Mr. *Pen-*
nyman (who was a Quaker about Twenty Years) and the
Quakers, was the Falfe Returns of their Collections, from
the feveral Counties in *England*, of the *Sufferings* of the
Friends, and Entring them (tho' proved to be Falfe) in
their General Regifter of Sufferings at *London*, For this
they (to quiet Mr. *Pennyman*, and others, who Exclaimed
againft this, as a great Deceit) made a fhew as if they
would turn off the Clerk of this Regifter, one *Ellis Hooks*,
but, as we are informed, they did not turn him off.

13.
Whereas they
have publifhed
of late Tears,
feveral Confef-
fions of their
Faith, which
feem to be much
more agreeable
to the Word of
God, and more

Joseph Wyeth, in his *Primitive Chriftianity continued,*
Printed 1698. *p.* 6. Afferts thus, ' Our Principles are NOW
' no other then what they were when we were firft a Peo-
' ple, for Truth Changes not. And *pag.* 53. he repeats it
again, faying, ' That our Principles are N O W no other
' then what they were when firft a People.
And in their Yearly Epiftle, Printed 1696. they fay,
' We

(27)

' We cannot but Recommend unto you, the holding up *confirmable to the belief of the Church of England, than formerly, we have just cause to dif-* ' the Holy Teſtimony of Truth, which had made us to be ' a People; and that in all the parts of it, for TRUTH ' is one, and CHANGES not.

And in *The Quakers Cleared*, Printed——*p.7.* they ſpeak *truſt theſe their Profeſſions, as being deſigned to Serve a Turn, becauſe they are ſo far from diſ-owning their Ancient Books, in which theſe Blaſphemies are contained, that* thus, *God is the ſame, Truth is the ſame, his People the ſame, and their Principles the ſame.*

And for Concluſion, *Geo. Whitehead*, in his Brief Remarks on *T. C's* Book annext to the *Counterfeit Convert*, Printed 1694. *p.* 72. ſaith, *I may ſee Cauſe, otherwiſe to Word the Matter, and yet our Intentions be the ſame.*

they tell us, they have not deviated from any one Point of Doctrine which they firſt held.

A Poſtſcript *by another Hand to the* Quakers.

Friends,

HAVING obſerved your Timerouſneſs about the Petition, ſince I came to Town, I take leave to tell you, that it ſeems to me, to ariſe from a ſenſible Knowledge and Conviction of your Errors; tho' you have the boldneſs to Impoſe upon the World in your late Book, *An Apology for the Quakers, and an Appeal to the Inhabitants of* Norfolk, *&c.* to ſay, *Who can Convict us of any Errors in Fundamentals?* &c. Who can? I can : I have : And, God willing, ſhall continue to do it ſtill, unleſs you Retract them : And ſo have many others ; and this you are deeply ſenſible of, elſe you would not be ſo ſtartled and affrighted becauſe of the Petition, which neither Incite to Perſecution, nor any Alteration of the Act of Toleration of Proteſtant Diſſenters ; but only, *That the Quakers Principles and Practices may be ſtrictly Examined and Cenſured, or Suppreſt ; as they* (upon Examination) *ſhall appear to deſerve ; and as to the Wiſdom of the Government ſhall ſeem meet,* &c. This is the Subſtance of what is deſired in the Petition, which doth ſo ſtartle you, which is a great ſign, that you are Convicted of Errors in Fundamentals : You formerly blamed others for flying to the Powers of the Earth, as a ſign that they had loſt the Lord, *p.* 18. calling the Parliament the Beaſt that carry the Whore, yet now none are ſo induſtriouſly concerned, nor more tedious in their ſolicitations to the Parliament, than the Quakers, *Sic mutantur.*

As for your Term, *Apoſtate,* which you often throw upon me, and others ; 'tis no more than you caſt upon all People, (read the 16 page herein) that Love, Own, and Honour the King, yea, any King, ſince the Apoſtles time ; and thereby charge all to be Apoſtates, and in the Apoſtacy ; whether Lords and Commons in Parliament, Judges, Juſtices, *&c.* Yea, both Clergy and Laity of all Ranks and Degrees, who either are or have been Loyal to this, or any other King, in any Age ſince the Days of the Apoſtles ; all are by your Ancient Teſtimony *Apoſtates ;* and the Kings are with you *Spiritual Egyptians.* Theſe are your Primitive Principles you came into the World withal ; which in your Yearly Meetings, or Convocations, as well as in your late Prints, you Revive and Renew in all its parts, and tell us you are not changed : Only *G. Whitehead* in your Name, ſays, *We may ſee cauſe otherwiſe to word the Matter, and yet our Intentions the ſame,* &c. as above quoted : And that your Principles are now no other (notwithstanding your new late Creeds to the contrary) than what they were when first a People; and what your Principles then were, here is both Authors produced, Book, Page and Line. What can you defire more ? They do not go behind your Backs to Try, Judge and Condemn you ; when you challeng'd them, they met you, and would have proved their Charge upon you but to my Knowledge (being prefent) you refufed to own your Books, or the Doctrines therein contained, or make any Defence to the Charge upon you : I fay, they did not go behind your Backs, to Try, Judge, and Condemn you, as you have done them. See *Burroughs's* Works, *P.* 223. *viz. A juft and lawful Trial of the Teachers and Minifters of this Age,* (Reprinted 1672.) *by a perfect proceeding againft them, and they are Righteoufly examined, Juftly weighed, Truly meafured, and Condemned to be contrary to all the Minifters of Chrift in former Ages; and to Agree and Concurr with all the falfe Prophets and Deceivers; and being brought to the* (Quakers) *Bar of Juftice, thefe things are truly charged, and legally proved upon them, and found Guilty,* &c.

Now Friends confider, and be cool, do you think this was fair Dealing in you, thus to condemn the Clergy of all Ranks at once ? If not, how can you have the Face to go to the Bifhops for Favour, until you have retracted thefe your abomina-

ble Antient Teftimonies, Printed in 1657, and Reprinted 1672. And you tell us you are the fame ftill, only you can word the Matter otherwife. I know I anger you, for bringing to Light your hidden Works of Darknefs; and 'tis for that you account me unreafonable: But if it be unreafonable in me to Recite thefe your Clandeftine Trials, Judgments and Sentences of the Clergy behind their Backs, (and a Hundred more of your horrible Tenents) how much more unreafonable are your old Prophets, and prefent Teachers, who firft writ and publifh'd thefe things, and now juftifie and defend them?

Again, This your Prophet and Son of Thunder, in his Works, *P.* 273. tells the World, that the Sufferings of the *Quakers* are greater, yea, and more unjuft too, than the Sufferings in the Days of Chrift his Apoftles and Martyrs; yea, all the Ten Perfecutions, by your Doctrin, were nothing to the *Quakers* Sufferings. See Page 26. herein. But that I may fhew the Vanity of this your Prefumption, as well as the *Quakers* Defign, I fhall once more give a Hint of the Nature of the Sufferings of the *Quakers,* and of the Apoftles and Martyrs, and let the World judge what Principles you came into the World withal. In order to which, take this fhort Parallel.

Of the Quakers *Sufferings, fee their Book, ftiled,* A horrible thing committed in the Land, *&c.* Page 8. *Taken from* Robert Minter, *the 4th. of the 4th. Month,* 1658. *by Prieft* Alexander Bradley, *of Elmfton, in* Kent.

Firft, Two Feather-Beds.
Three Bolfters, and one Pillow.
One Flock-bed and Bolfter.
One Bedftead and Curtains.
Iron Rods and Cords for two Beds.
Ten pair of Sheets, and one Rug.
Five Table-cloths, and fix Towels.
One Dozen of Trenchers, and one Spade.
A Mattock and Dung-fork.
45 double Clouts for a Child.

Of the Sufferings of the Apoftles and Martyrs, as I find them in Hift. John Baptift, *St.* Stephen, *St.* James, Philip, Andrew, Matthew, Mark, *&c*

Some of whom were flee'd alive.
Some their Brains knockt out.
Some Crucified.
Some burn'd alive.
Some put in Boiling Oil, and the like.
Again, One hang'd, and her Skin flee'd off.
One had his Tongue cut out.
One broken in a Mortar.
One put in a Cauldron of boiling Oil.
One fry'd in a Pan.
One whipt, and her Dugs cut off.
Some bound to Axle-trees and burnt.
Some thrown to Lions and Tygers, *&c.*
Some tofs'd on the Horns of wild Bulls.
Some

12 Beds and 4 Blankets.
Six Caps for a Woman.
Two Neckcloths, and four double Crofs-cloths for a Woman.
One Mantle and feven Chin-ftays.
Three Shirts and three Biggins.
A Swadling-band and Back-band.
Two double Bibs and one Dreffing.
Three Bufhels of Barley.
Three Milk-Pails, and half a Cheefe.
Three Forms, and two Tables.
Three Pin-cufheons and Pins.
Befides a Thoufand Pins more, &c.

Some their Brains beat out with Clubs.
Some burn'd at Stakes.
Some prefs'd to Death with Lead.
Some hang'd on Gibbets.
Some hang'd on Trees till dead.
Some hewn in pieces with Swords.
Some fawn in pieces.
Some Womens Bellies ript up.
Some torn in pieces with wild Horfes.
Some hung on Tenter-hooks till dead.
Some hang'd by the Hair till dead.
Some had their Nofes and Ears cut off.
Some their Mouths flit to their Ears, &c.

Thus much by way of Parallel; the Dif proportion I leave to your Confideration; not to mention your Sham-Sufferings, as that of Sam. Cater, who pretended, and got it recorded, that he fuffer'd 20 l for Preaching at Phakenham in Norfolk, when he fuffer'd not a Penny; but by his Subtilty got 10 l. fent him from their Fund at London, as at large elfewhere I have fhewed. I come next to fhew your way of Canonizing your Saints, and what Perfons they are you Canonize; and I think Rome do not outdo you; as alfo your Defign to render our Magiftrates Infamous to Pofterity, in order to exalt your own Horn. For in another Book,ftiled, A Word of Reproof to my Fellow Soldiers, &c. Printed 1659 P. 79. you fay, ' Here fol-' loweth fome Signs, Examples and Judg-' ments for the Accurfed Generation, who ' defire a Sign,but they are Miracles to them ' that believe. And (faith E. B.) let fuch reach hither their Hands, and with me feel and fe the Wounds that the Lord of Life hath received in his Members, &c.

1. In Suffex, Prieft Coffine caufed Tho. Leacock to be Imprifoned for fpeaking a few Words after he had done; and foon after the Prieft was cut off by Death.

2. J hn Chatfield, Prieft of Horfham, caufed Tho. Leacock to be Imprifoned; who foon after fell into a Dropfie, and in Six Months died.

3. Prieft Cutfly of Arundel, being Inftrumental in Tho. Leacock's Perfecution, fuddainly after died.

4. Edward Hunt, Norwich Goaler, who after G. Whitehead was difcharged, brought his Action againft him for Four Pence a Night, foon after cut off by Death.

5. Rob. Al in of Buk, who abufed Tho. Morford in the Street, had a Boy fcall'd to,

Death; and Parfon Fenk beat Chrif. Atkinfon.
Reader, Here is a few of the Examples, there being about 80 more in 9 Years in England and Wales, and ftill they are collecting, elfe how will they outftrip Rome? It remains now to fhew what manner of Saints thefe are you now Canonize; and for whom thefe Judgments and miraculous Wonders were wrought.

1. Tho. Leacock, your Teacher, was a great Drinker; who on a time, at a Gentleman's Houfe in Emny, near Wisbech, drank till he was fo drunk, that going out to make Water, fell backward into a Rain Ciftern, brake his Bladder, was forced to carry a Difh in his Breeches, to catch his Water, who foon after died miferably. But whether in Judgment for your Prefumption, his own Sins, or a Warning to others, I will not determine, left therein I turn Quaker again.

2. Tho. Murford was a more vile Perfon; who being one of your Teachers, pretended to be a Surgeon, and applied Remedies to the Female Sex where he ought not; many in Norwich can give you a larger Account than I will do here.

3. G. Whitehead is ftill living; and I could be glad he would Improve his Time, by feeking Repentance while it may be found, for his great Sin, in making a Schifm in the Church, &c.

4. Chrif. Atkinfon, thus Canonized, and one of your Prophets, Companion to G. Whitehead, in Writing, Printing, Preaching, Travelling, and Suffering, got a Wench with Child at Norwich, tried fince for Felony, and hang'd; one of your now Teachers of Fame amongft you gave me an Account lately of his Execution.

G   Eut

But as this shew your Design not good, thus to record such Trifles, even to a Row of Pins and a Double Clout, so is it wicked with a Witness to Record such as Persecutors who execute the Laws ; and that such as die after, it is in Judgment; and Presumptuous in you, to sit in the Judgment-Seat.

But why should your being examin'd about these and the like Infolencies, put such a Dread upon you, and thus startle you, since it is agreeable to your own Proposition in *Burrough*'s Epistle to his Works, who thus wrote? *viz.* 'And so gladly would ' we (*Quakers*) be made manifest to all the ' World; that if any, especially the Heads ' and Rulers have any Doubts concerning ' us. For that End, let any propound that ' we, with the Consent of Authority, 10, ' 20, or more of us, give as many of the ' ablest Priests and Professors a Meeting for ' Dispute at any Place and Time, and for ' what Continuance they please—— Let the ' Priests and Professors object what they can ' against us, our Principles, Practices, and ' whole Religion; and let such that cannot ' prove our selves of the true Church and ' Religion, but is found in Error, let such ' deny their Worship and Religion, and ' renounce it under their Hands, and con- ' fess they have been deceived, &c.

I find in another Book of yours to the same Purpose, intituled, *The Copies of several Letters written by sundry Friends, as they were moved by the Holy Ghost*, &c. Printed 1660. where *Geo. Whitehead* in his Admonition to King *Charles* II. *P.* 53. hath these Words: ' And if any of the Priests do Inform the ' King against the People call'd *Quakers*, or ' against our Princip'es, it is but a reason- ' able thing that thou hear both Parties Face ' to Face, that we may answer them ; this ' was upon me to lay before the King, that ' we are free to vindicate *any* Principle we ' hold, according to Scripture.

Now for your Friends at *West Dereham*; to avoid the force of these Arguments, when urged, as a Reason for you to defend your selves from the Charge the Clergy exhibited against you, pursuant to your Challenge, as that they were written 25 or 30 Years since; this could be no Argument, since you pretend to write from the Mouth of the Lord, moved thereto by the Holy Ghost. And as such, of greater Authority than the Bible, for the Writings of *Moses* and the Prophets, Christ and the Apostles, are much older, yet still full of Force: But this your Shuffle shew'd the Justices of Peace, the Gentry and Clergy, as well as the Protestant Dissenters, that your Principles are so destructive to common Christianity, as that they did not dare to stand the Test ; and this, yea, ONLY this, so far as I know, put them upon a Petition to the Honourable House of Commons, to do that for God and the Christian Religion, which they could not do; namely, to examine your Principles, and censure your Errors, as to their Wisdom should see meet: And in this, they (both Church of *England*-Men and Protestant Dissenters)areUnanimous; and this disturbs you, this perplexes you, and for this your Tool, *John Field*, call and compare them to *Herod* and *Pilate*, *Hamou* and *Judas* : And say *Field*, *Do not blame till you examine*. I tell you they have examined, and therefore blame, and they find your Blasphemies so Great, so Apparent, and Manifest, that they also desire their Superiors to examine; and when they have so done, no doubt but they'll blame and censure your Errors : And this startles you, this makes you look about you, and cry Persecution, Persecution, when no Body designs it ; nay, no Body desires it ; for that's the Way to encrease you, who are for Boldness like a Flint Stone, which lay it on a Table, and smite it with a Hammer, and it will abide Obdurate ; but lay it on a soft Cusheon, and a little Stroke will make it fly into many Shivers.

And though none solicite against your having the same Liberty that other Dissenters have, yet I must say there is not the same Reason for you to expect it : For when the *Baptists* in your dear Friend *Oliver Cromwell*'s time had said, *They thought it their Duty to preserve them* [*i. e.* Bishops and Clergy] *from all Violence*, your Teachers Assaulted them from all Quarters, even for so much as Tenderness towards the Bishops, as to preserve their Persons from Violence and Injuries, much more for thinking of granting them any Toleration.

Edward Burroughs, your great Prophet and Primitive Pillar, wrote a Tract on purpose against this Declaration of the *Bap.ists*, and says to them, (*P.* 618. of his Works, as Reprinted 1672.) *What! Are you about to make*

make a League and Covenant with Anti-christ? —— Do you look upon them to be Ministers of Christ, or of Antichrist? And P. 619. What are you now for Tolerating Episcopacy? And if Episcopacy, why may not Popery be tolerated, seeing they are one and the same in Ground and Nature, &c. He was seconded by another of your Teachers of great Name amongst you, viz. Richard Hubberthorne, in his Works, Reprinted 1663.—who also attacked this Declaration of the Baptists, P. 229. of his Works, saying, Why will you not tolerate Popery as well as Episcopacy? Have not the Professors of Episcopacy murthered and slain, and do labour to murther and slay the People of God, as well as the Papists? And will you tolerate the Common-Prayer among the Episcopacy, and not the Mass-Book among the Papists; seeing that the Mass was the Substance out of which the Common-Prayer was extracted? &c.

And much more to the same purpose in these and others of your Early Writers, which shew sufficiently your Antient Principles, and you tell us they are now no other than what they were when you were first a People, as in my Books I have more largely set forth, which may be had at Mr. Kettleby's, at the Bishops-Head, in St. Paul's Church-yard. And for the Truth of my Quotations, I am ready to justifie under the greatest Penalties my Superiors shall think fit to assign; and for my Arguments, every Man is left to his Judgment of Discretion, as I desire my self, and this may serve in Answer to all your Clamours; and what I have yet to say, you'll see in my next, which is ready for the Press, which is a Proof of my own Charge against you at West-Dereham Church in Norfolk, the 9th of December last: Where not only the Quakers were forced to confess the Truth of my Quotations, but four Clergymen of known Reputation have under their Hands certified the same. As to your scattering your Books both in the Church and the Country round, it is in Obedience to G. Fox's Doctrine and Example, in his Book, The Vials of the Wrath of God, &c. Printed 1655. P. 2. This [Book] is to be scattered among the Ignorant, Simple, and Blind People, &c. I am satisfied your Antient Testimony was design'd to bring the Clergy to a Morsel of Bread, but hitherto you have been disappointed: For, says G. Fox in his Paper concerning Poets, &c. P. 8. But I shall

tell you the Scholars of Oxford and Cambridge, It would be more pleasing to God, for you to get a Spade on your Backs, and a great old Glove, and a Bill in your Hand, and stop Gaps, and make up old Hedges, and thresh out Corn, and go amongst Day-labouring Men for 3 d. a Day, &c. And indeed if it be as Burrough's, their great Prophet, said in the recited Trial and Condemnation of the Clergy, in his Works, P. 223, 227, 234, viz. That they Agree and Concur with all the false Prophets and Deceivers in former Ages; that they are Ministers of Antichrist; and for which all honest People have left them, yet have 1500000 l. a Year for their Antichristian Service, as his Antient Testimony sets forth, Printed 1655. and Reprinted by the Approbation of Geo. Whitehead, &c. 1672. then indeed 3 d. a Day is enough; nay, too much. But that this Antient Testimony (from which they say they do not deviate) might be renewed, and kept fresh in Memory, W. Penn in his Guide mistaken, &c. Printed 1668. P. 18. saith, Whilst the idle Gormandizing Priests of England run away with above 1500000 l. a Year, under Pretence of being God's Ministers; and that no sort of People have been so universal'y through Ages the very Bane of Soul and Body to the Universe, ae that Abominable Tribe, for whom the Theatre of God's most Dreadful Vengeance is reserved to all their Eternal Tragedy upon, &c. And if so, it's time for them to get a Bill, a great Glove, mend Gaps, and Thresh for 3 d. a Day, as their Apostle Fox prescrib'd.

But J. Feild in his Book, An Apology for the Quakers, and an Appeal to the Inhabitants of Norfolk and Suffolk, &c. P. 9. 1st. Would the Clergymen account it just, that any should Charge them, Condemn and Censure them. 2dly, They exhort, To do to others as they would that others should do to them. 3dly, P. 5. We (say they) pray for all Men, for Kings, and all that are in Authority. 4thly, p. 7. We (say the Quakers) have, and always had a high Value for the Scriptures above all other Books. 5thly, p. 1. They (i. e. Clergy) Incense those in Authority against this Innocent People (i. e. Quakers) that the Monster of Persecution might be again raised to Suppress them, &c.

Ans. As to the First, Would the Clergy account it just to Charge and Condemn them? &c. Just or unjust, they are both Charged and Condemned at the Quakers Bar, as above quoted; yea, and in *Smith's* Works, P. 157, 161. the *Quakers* Dialogu'd the Bifhops, and fummon'd all Ecclefiaftical Courts and Officers; and not only by their Authority Condemn them, but call the Bifhops Monfters, and into the Bargain fay, *The Book of Common-Prayer is conceived by an Adulterous Womb, and that it receives its Strength from the Pope's Loins.* And 2*dly, That therein you* (Quakers) *do not do as you would be done by*; and therein grofs Hypocrites and Diffemblers with God and Man. But 3*d'y*, your Pretence *to pray for all Men, for Kings*, &c. This is fo Falfe and Falacious, that I challenge the wholeWorld to produce one Inftance of your praying for King*!William*,or anyKing,fave once at aMeeting at *Mildin-Hall*, where *Sam. Cater* prayed for the late K. *J.* II. and how fhould you be found in that Practice, fince all Kings (with you) are but Spiritual *Egyptians*, by your Ancient Teftimony, from which you,have not deviated in one Point? But your Principles the fame they ever were, tho' as *Whitehead* fays, *You can now read the Matter otherwife.* 4thly, *That you value the Scriptures above any Books in the World.* This is falfe with a witnefs, when you in Print tell us, *We may as well burr the Bible as your Writings,* (fee p 9. herein) calling the Scriptures *Duft, Death, Serpents Meat, Beaftly Ware,* and that *Preaching out of them is Conjuration.* And *G. Whitehead* tells us in his Book, *Truth defending the Quakers,*&c. p. 7. That *what is fpoken from the Spirit of Truth in any, is of greater Authority than the Bible.* And many of your Books (nay, even that) are faid to be given forth from the Spirit of Truth, the Ho'y Ghoft, and fpoken from the Mouth of the Lord. How then do you value the Bible above all Books in the World? But as *Solomon* faid, *Prov.* 26. 3 *A Whip for the Horfe, a Bridle for the Afs, and a Rod for the Fool's Back*; and fo you muft give me leave to whip this *John Feild* for his deep Hypocrifie and Deceit; and I wifh it may do him Good. What! to pretend that the *Quakers* value the Bible above all Books, then confequently above their own. This is fuch a Lie. that it ftabs it felf; when you exalt and va'ue your own as of greater Authority, and are commanded by your Teachers to read them in your Meetings, and never read a Chapter of the Old and New Teftament in your Religious Meetings, (if fuch I may

F I N I S.

call them) fince you were a People; neither is it agreeable to your Ancient Teftimony. Nay, I am perfwaded, that fhould the Government think fit, for a Proof of your Sincerity herein, to injoin you to read a Chapter of the Bible at the beginning of your Meeting, (I mean, by fuch of your Teachers as can read a Chapter) you would be fo far from fubmitting to Authority, that they'd firft go to Jayl, and then call it Perfecution, and record it to Pofterity: But would it therefore ever the more be Perfecution? I trow not; fince it was the Practice of Jewifh, as well as the Chriftian Church in all Ages of the World. But 5*thly* and *laft'y, That the Petitioners would Incenfe thefe in Authority to raife that Monfter, Perfecution, upon you.* Now, tho' I do profefs my felf a Member of the Church of *England*,*I have often, and do now again tell you, that I am againft Perfecution, and will add, that Perfecution for the Name of Jefus, or for Righteoufnefs fake, is a Badge of a falfe Church; of which, your Schifm in *Penfilvania* has given a Demonftration. And had you Power in your Hand (which God grant you may not) I doubt not but we fhould foon feel your litt'e Finger as heavy, as ever you felt a Parliaments Loins. Witnefs your Indicting me for Printing, unlicenced; your own frequent Practice at that time,and yourPerfecuting of *G.Keith,&c.* in *Penfilvania*; but I hope all Suffering is not Perfecution. Shall Men fire Houfes, and poyfon Rivers, and not be Controuled, Limited, nay, Punifhed, if they will follow their own Light,b'ind Zeal and Imaginations. In like manner, fuch as poyfon the Streams of the Chriftian Religion, fubvert the Faith, undermine Chriftianity, broach and maintain Heretical Opinions, and Damnab'e Errors, even denying the Lord that bought them, as you have in Print, which I take to be a Fundamental Error; and by me proved upon you; I hope then it wi'l not be raifing Perfecution, to have you examined about thefe things; which is the main thing you fear, whi'lt you make the World believe you fear Perfecution.

Thus referring *John Feild* to my former Books, I fubfcribe my felf the *Quakers* Friend, tho' I tell them the Tru'h,

Feb 18.
1698.

Francis Bugg.